The Lighter Side of...

TENNIS

KT-433-161

SeTo
PUBLISHING

THE LIGHTER SIDE OF TENNIS

ISBN 0 908697 36 8
© Copyright SeTo Publishing Ltd 1989

SeTo Publishing Ltd
PO Box 4028
Auckland 1
New Zealand

Printed in Hong Kong through Colorcraft

...AND WHILE I'M AT IT, I'D LIKE TO THANK THE BALL BOYS FOR THEIR CHEERFUL SMILES AND QUICK RELEXES.
Slazenger

BET YOU CAN'T JUGGLE A TENNIS RACKET WITH ONE HAND BEHIND YOUR BACK!
adidas

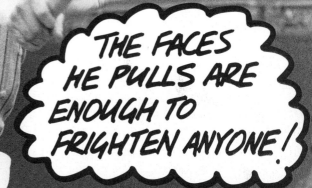

YOU'D MISS SHOTS, TOO... IF YOU HAD TO PLAY WITH A MOP ON YOUR HEAD!

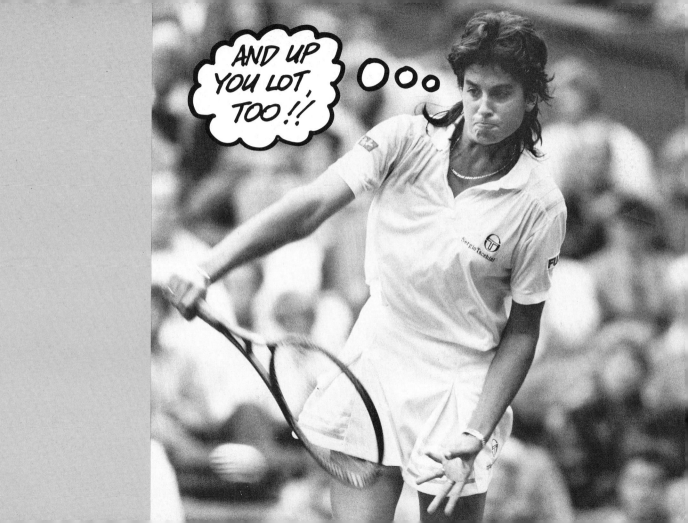